REACH

DON'T BE ORDINARY

AF536476

ONYEKANNA N. EGBUCHUNEM

Copyright © Onyekanna N. Egbuchunem
All Rights Reserved.

This book has been self-published with all reasonable efforts taken to make the material error-free by the author. No part of this book shall be used, reproduced in any manner whatsoever without written permission from the author, except in the case of brief quotations embodied in critical articles and reviews.

The Author of this book is solely responsible and liable for its content including but not limited to the views, representations, descriptions, statements, information, opinions and references ["Content"]. The Content of this book shall not constitute or be construed or deemed to reflect the opinion or expression of the Publisher or Editor. Neither the Publisher nor Editor endorse or approve the Content of this book or guarantee the reliability, accuracy or completeness of the Content published herein and do not make any representations or warranties of any kind, express or implied, including but not limited to the implied warranties of merchantability, fitness for a particular purpose. The Publisher and Editor shall not be liable whatsoever for any errors, omissions, whether such errors or omissions result from negligence, accident, or any other cause or claims for loss or damages of any kind, including without limitation, indirect or consequential loss or damage arising out of use, inability to use, or about the reliability, accuracy or sufficiency of the information contained in this book.

Made with ♥ on the Notion Press Platform
www.notionpress.com

To everyone in pursuit of greatness

Contents

Preface

One of the thoughts I have had to ponder on so frequently in life is: "No individual has the right to come into this world and go out of it without leaving behind him distinct and legitimate reasons for having passed through it".

The first man to walk on the Moon left his foot print indelibly on the moon and will be remembered throughout history. You have an opportunity to do the same, although it may not be walking on the moon. How, you may wonder? Through a DREAM!

The idea of having a man on the Moon was a dream in someone's mind. Although at its conception, it may have seemed impossible, but it has been achieved. Today, the world is witnessing scientific and technological breakthroughs in the field of medicine, engineering, robotics, etc. because of ideas.

Anything is possible! You just have to dream it.

A dream is that idea, that vision that burns within you. They are the visions of what you want to do, what you want your life to be at its highest level of fulfillment.

The good news is that everyone can dream. You see, God has given everyone the infinite capacity to dream. A dream is the blueprint of what God wants you to manifest in the realm of reality so as to impact your world. Without a dream, we would all live un-impactful lives.

Most people have lost their dream simply because they believed they were not born for something great in this world. There is nothing as farther away from the truth as this false belief.

It is not just enough to have a dream; you must know how to implement it—to move ahead with it. If you want to successfully achieve you dream, you have to get your basics right. There are basic principles you must follow. These principles are pillars that will help you achieve your dream.

In reading the first chapter of the book of Joshua, the Holy Spirit showed me basic principles the LORD gave Joshua. Joshua was Moses' successor, and was saddled with the awesome responsibility of leading God's people to their inheritance.

God is sovereign and ever willing to guide us at every turn. And God did that by giving Joshua some instructions. Embedded in those instructions are principles which if applied would guarantee tremendous results. Joshua's success depended on his ability as well as his willingness to put those principles to good use.

Principles are universal and timeless. That means if it worked for Joshua, it sure will work for you. Although we all have dreams we would love to see fulfilled, not everyone is always willing to do what it takes to follow through. While most people quit at the first sign of resistance, some others never find the nerve to start. But there are others, just a few, who actually succeed.

I have discovered that whether or not people fulfill their dreams has nothing to do with their initial set of circumstances. I have read about certain individuals who were poor and disadvantaged, yet went on to accomplish great things. This book will show you that succeeding at that dream has nothing to do with your initial circumstances.

Over the years, I have attended countless seminars and conferences, read over a hundred books, listened to countless tapes on the subject of personal development and success. I have found these principles embodied in this book to be the key to accomplishing great things. When anyone embraces these basic principles, there is absolutely nothing he cannot accomplish.

The material in this book offers you step-by-step instructions of how you can make your life count. I can tell you this: this book is an investment. And you having it and reading it is an investment in yourself-an investment that is certain to pay dividends when you apply the principles and take action.

Acknowledgements

As always, I was blessed to have the help and support of Reverend Vanessa Hinton and her husband Bishop Winfred Hinton. Thank you mom for your enthusiasm, and for working tirelessly, editing, proof reading, and pushing, to make this book a reality. I thank God for bringing me to you.

I want to express my profound gratitude to the wonderful people who have shaped my life by their teachings: John C. Maxwell, Bishop David Oyedepo, Pastor Chris Oyakhilome, Gloria Copeland and Joyce Meyers

CHAPTER ONE

YOU NEED A DREAM

"Now it came to pass after the death of Moses the servant of Jehovah, that Jehovah spake unto Joshua the son of Nun, Moses' minister, saying, Moses my servant is dead; now therefore arise, go over this Jordan, thou and all this people, unto the land which I do give to them, even to the children of Israel"

(Joshua 1:1-2)

A dream has the ability to command destinies

All successful endeavors begin with a dream. A dream of what we hope to accomplish in life is the foundation for success. Without a dream of what you want to accomplish with your life, your chances of realizing success is significantly reduced.

Can you really define at this point what matters to you? Do you have a personal dream for your life? I am not talking about making money here; rather I'm referring to that thing which will make your life count. The truth is, you will never live a life that truly counts until you define what truly matters to you.

The fundamental key to living a life that counts is a dream. If you do not already have one, then you must get one. Dreams that capture our imaginations and inspire our deepest wills begin in the very mind of God. In other words, you must ask God for a dream. This is where the journey begins; spend time necessary to capture a dream for your life.

Without a clear dream you'll be unable to live your life with intention. Intentionality is purpose driven; and a dream is the path to purpose.

Most people I have met have a vague notion that there is something they would love to do someday, but have no idea what it is. Does this describe you? You see, clarity is important; your ability to describe in great details what you would wish to accomplish or become is vital to success.

God is given to clarity; He doesn't want you to live by vague notions but by clarity. That's why He instructs without ambiguity:

"...write the vision, and make it plain upon tables that he may run that readeth it: the vision is yet for an appointed time, but at the end it shall speak and not lie: though it tarry, wait for it, because it will surely come, it will not tarry" -Habakkuk 2:2-3

Writing your dreams or visions of what you want to accomplish is the first and vital step towards fulfilling your dreams. Any dream or vision for your future for which you cannot describe in great details and with enthusiasm will be lost.

At this point, I'd like to give perspective to what a dream or vision should be.

A dream is the seed of your life's purpose embedded in your soul which draws you to pursue a unique path to accomplish that purpose.

A dream is an inspiring picture of the future you're designed to fulfill. A dream is so powerful that it commands destinies. I believe it is God's precious gift to human beings.

What makes a dream compelling is purpose. If a dream does not fulfill purpose then it can't be regarded as compelling. When we know why we are here, we come alive. A dream or a vision is clarity as to your purpose in life.

Have you ever struggled with the thoughts that your life may not be headed in the direction you want? Or maybe you're unaware of where your life may be headed? Either way, you've not discovered why you are here.

Ephesians 2:10 says,

"For we are his workmanship, created in Christ Jesus for good works which God prepared beforehand so that we would walk in them"

Think about that! God created us with purpose. He filled us with unique gifts, talents and strengths to accomplish something extraordinary with our lives. A dream or vision therefore is the picture of your purpose which God has placed in your heart to manifest.

Purpose is really what defines our usefulness and consequently our contributions.

A dream or a vision helps us make valuable contributions while propelling us forward. My purpose in writing this book is to encourage you to dream and pursue you dream.

I have met so many people who like Joseph in the Bible had great dreams but were discouraged from pursuing their dreams. I too was discouraged by people as well as disappointing failures, until I read the incredible story of Wilbur and Orville Wright.

What was so amazing about these brothers? Well, the Wright brothers accomplished something that the vast majority of people-even the most educated-had not believed to be possible—flight!

Their dream of building a functional airplane was challenged by critics who said it could not be done. The lack of funding as well as several failed experiments discouraged their dream. However, in spite of the many discouragements, they relentlessly pursued their dream.

This story and many others, reveal that Man can accomplish anything if he has a dream, as well as a will strong enough to pursue it. The Bible says, 'all things are possible to him that believes' (Mark 9:23)

The Wright brothers dream and their persistent pursuit of it revolutionized Transportation as we know it today.

The dissenting voices of discouragement have always been all through history, and are still here today.

In building the Ark, Noah too was discouraged by the people of his day. The Ark was a laughable project given that they had never seen a single drop of rain, much less a deluge. Noah didn't lose hope; he did not give in to discouragement.

There was Nehemiah, whose dream was to rebuild the fallen walls of Jerusalem. Certain men arose to discourage him and put an end to his dream.

"And it came to pass that when Samballat heard that we builded the wall, he was wroth, and took great indignation, and mocked the Jews. And he spoke before his brethren and the army of Samaria, and said, what do these feeble Jews? Will they fortify themselves? Will they sacrifice? Will they make an end in a day? Will they revive the stones out of the heaps of the rubbish which are burned? Now Tobiah the Amonite was by him, and said, even that which they build, if a fox go up, he shall even break down their stone wall" (Nehemiah 4:1-3)

Have you experienced something like that? You're so excited at your dream that you shared it with someone and their response sucked the air right out of you leaving you flat out.

Great dreams have died at the hands of discouraging voices. Such voices are tasked with the responsibility of killing dreams. These people could be friends, family, or persons of outstanding educational qualifications, who will tell you your dream is impossible, it cannot be done; no one has ever tried it. If they're generous enough, they will bluntly tell you: you will fail!

Have you ever had anyone try to discourage your dream? Or even laughed at you when you told them your dream?

Well do not listen to them and don not give up. Let their reaction become a motivation for you to succeed; let it inflame your passion.

Over the years, I have come to understand that most of the time when someone tries to discourage you from your dream, it usually is because they have given up on their dream or they are simply threatened by you.

There are a number of reasons why people give up on their dreams; the fear of failure, lack of self-discipline, a lack of confidence among other things.

The point is this: do not allow anyone who gave up on their dream stop you from reaching yours.

Besides the people who crush our dreams, there is also the part where we give up on our dream just because we failed in our initial attempt to accomplishing it. When next you feel like quitting just because you failed, you will do well to remember the man Thomas Edison the great inventor. Among his several inventions, most notable was the light bulb. But, did you know before he succeeded, he had close to a thousand failed experiments?

The Wright brothers also had many failed and disappointing experiments before they finally succeeded.

When something goes wrong in an attempt to accomplish our dreams, we often give up saying, 'well, that's the end of that, I'm not going to do it again; at least I tried'.

That's a terrible thing to do!

Failing once is not a good judge of your potential. Neither is failing twice or even a hundred times. Think about it: if you fell while trying to walk, how would you expect to get to where you want to go if you gave up?

Moses made that same mistake when he failed in his initial attempt at liberating Israel. It resulted in his fleeing to Midian, only to be tending his Father-in-law's sheep. He gave up his dream for close to 40 years until God brought him back on track. Although, he tried advancing excuses why he could not, God would not have any of it.

"Come now therefore and I will send thee into Pharaoh, that thou mayest bring forth my people the children of Israel out of Egypt. And Moses said unto God, who am I that I should go unto Pharaoh and that I should bring forth the children of Israel out of Egypt?" Exodus 3:10-12, AMP King James

If you have lost your confidence and are afraid to go at your dream, consider this book an intervention of some sort, urging you to revive your dream and go at it again.

In case you haven't noticed, failure is a vital part of success, and a part of our human development. We all encounter failure at some point in our bid to accomplishing something; In fact, more failures than successes. But the good thing is that failure is an essential growth opportunity. We grow from our experiences of failure, and not from our successes.

Thomas Edison was credited as saying after his failed experiments, 'I have discovered 999 ways in which not to make a light bulb'.

If you have failed at trying to reach your dream and you are afraid of trying again, then that should give you concerns. In as much as God is interested in your success, he is equally interested in how you handle failure. In the words of Abraham Lincoln: 'my concern is not whether you failed, but whether you are content with failure'.

I strongly agree that if you are unable to successfully handle failure, then you do not deserve to be successful! Never see failure as a dead end, but as finding another way to succeed. If you have lost sight of your dream, I encourage you to reconnect with it.

Keep your dream alive

You have the awesome responsibility of keeping your dream alive. Dreams, if not kept alive will die as the days go by. Daily work tasks and other urgent matters can choke your dreams thereby making you lose your initial passion and ultimately giving up on your dream.

One way of keeping your dream alive is to write it down. Not writing down your dream will narrow your chances at achieving them. Putting down your dream in writing is the vital step to achieving it. Notice what the Bible says:

"And the LORD answered me, and said, write the vision, and make it plain upon tables, that he may run that readeth it. For the vision is yet for an appointed time but at the end it shall speak and not lie, though it tarry, wait for it, because it will surely come, it will not tarry"Habakkuk 2:2-3, KJV

Although the fulfillment of your dream may take ample time, it has been found that writing them down on paper greatly aids focus and making helpful choices at a conscious and subconscious level.

Any dream, no matter how grandeur that you do not take the time to write down will be lost.

Having put down your dream on paper, the next thing is to place it where you can see it regularly. A constant reminder is necessary otherwise it will be forgotten. As you look at your dream on that paper, you will begin to flesh out the details, how you will actually achieve it. Every detail you add brings clarity and strengthens your resolve which will enable you to decide exactly where to begin.

Seeing your dream right before you every day is a great way to stay motivated and accountable for what you have set out to achieve.

Visualization is a great concept that allows you to train and stretch the mind to make room for the manifestation of your dream. Every time you see that paper, the image is impressed on your subconscious mind.

Most people still do not understand how powerful their minds are. You see, the mind is so powerful that it can turn a thought or belief into an experience.

Every time you look at your dream on paper, an image forms in your mind; and as you keep looking and thinking about it the stronger and clearer it becomes. Possibilities begin to form in your mind.

All God had to do to get Abraham to understand what he was trying to say was to show him:

"And Abram said, Lord God, what wilt thou give me, seeing I go childless, and the steward of my house is this Eliezer of Damascus? And Abram said, behold to me thou has given no seed, lo, one born in my house is mine heir.

And behold the word of the LORD came unto him, saying, this shall not be thine heir, but he that shall come out of thine own bowels shall be thine heir. And he brought him forth abroad and said, look now toward heaven, and tell the stars, if thou be able to number them, and he said unto him, so shall thy seed be" -Genesis 15:2-5

The principle is simple yet powerful: as long as your mind's eye can see it then you can have it. As long as the image is ingrained in your mind, everything will cooperate to help you bring it into reality.

One striking thing I noticed about the Wright brothers was that they connected with people who shared the same passion as they had; people who had done some work in their area of interest. If you want to keep your dream alive, talk and mix with people who share similar interests with you. The key here is to maintain your 'fire'.

Another way of keeping your dream alive is by reading. You read to get inspired at the same time improving yourself. When you read up on other people's success story, you will be inspired and motivated.

Keep your dreams in front of you. Think about it constantly. Meditate on it and the ways you can accomplish it. Imagine the life you desire, and the difference you can make in your world. Do not lose your motivation and drive; keep pressing forward with your dream.

CHAPTER TWO

LET GOD HELP YOU

"As I was with Moses, so I will be with you; I will never leave you nor forsake you"

Joshua 1:5

We live in a world where people are becoming increasingly independent most especially when it comes to their relationship with God. Everywhere you turn is a message that promotes the culture of increasing independence of Man from his maker.

Some people have trouble depending on anyone. Usually it stems from being hurt or disappointed—someone significant who let them down, a close friend or spouse who betrayed a trust. So they find themselves thinking 'I do not need anyone. I can make it on my own'.

I actually feel sorry for anyone who thinks he does not need God's assistance in his life. When you think you do not need God's help in accomplishing that dream, it could mean one or both of these: your dream is too small that it does not scare you. Or you are just too stubborn to ask for help.

Any dream that will make generational impact begins in the heart of God, and since it proceeds from him to man, it is always bigger than the man. When your dream is bigger than you, it will scare you. The size of your dream must frighten you when you compare it with your natural abilities and competences. Your dream must be big enough that it will require a miracle to accomplish it.

A dream for which God will be irrelevant in its accomplishment is small. I encourage you to have the kind of dream that will have generational impact. That is the kind of dream God puts in the hearts of anyone whose desire is to make an impact with their lives.

One point I need to clarify here is that the LORD didn't create man to be independent of him; certainly, no parent would love the idea of being trimmed out from their children's lives. If God gave you a dream to fulfill, don't you think he wants to be involved in its accomplishment?

From the very beginning, God created us to be divinely assisted. Think about the words He said to Joshua: 'as I was with Moses, I will be with you'. Moses accomplished extraordinary things because God assisted him. He surmounted challenges because God was with him. The good news is that this same promise is true for any of God's children today.

Your dreams won't just happen. You see, the first step in accomplishing your dream is a PLAN. You need to sit down on a regular basis and plan out a workable strategy for achieving that dream. A plan answers the vital question faced by all who have a dream—HOW?

How do I accomplish this dream?

This is where the great majority of people get hung up. There's nothing more frustrating than having a great idea but do not know just how to get it off!

The Bible notes:

"The labor of the foolish wearieth every one of them, because he knoweth not how to go to the city" -Ecclesiastes 10:15

Any vision, goal or dream no matter how great will die if you do not know how to go about it.

It is comforting to know that God has promised to help us in any area we let him. He is willing to provide us with guidance, wisdom, favor and strength we need to accomplish the dreams in our hearts. He is ever willing to assist us as long as we invite Him. This is a divine truth you should never forget. We must recognize that our success does not depend solely on our intellect or competence but, on the help that God provides us with.

Joshua's first task after crossing the River Jordan was taking Jericho, a tightly walled city. God showed up to assist Joshua in taking the city. His strategy was simple and very unconventional: Joshua and all his men were to march round the city every morning for 6 days, and 7 times on the seventh day, and with a long blast of the horn, they are to shout triumphantly.

This was not much a military strategy, not what a decorated General would have recommended. He would have gone with a more formidable approach like besieging the city, and hauling huge stones by catapults followed by archers firing flaming arrows.

God's methods may seem unconventional and most times, way too simple, that we'd doubt its possibility. God is vitally interested in your life and in your dreams. He wants to help make your dream a reality but, he will not be able to unless you open the door for him to do it.

One way God helps us is by providing guidance. Have you ever gone on a trip before to a place you've never been? Did you hire a guide or just decided to do it alone? If you decided to explore alone, it meant that you could do what you wanted to, but I believe you found out that it was not wise after all; you wasted so much time wandering aimlessly to find places yourself.

God is committed to help us with the fulfillment of our dreams by providing the much needed guidance. God has the road map for your life and that dream. The mistake most of us make is that we try so hard to follow other peoples' pattern in fulfilling our dreams. God has different plans and consequently different road maps for everyone. God's plan for you is quite different from mine; his road map for you is therefore unique.

Instead of wasting precious time trying to figure out how to fulfill your dream on your own, why don't you just seek his guidance.

Following a guide requires trusting someone or something other than yourself to lead the way. God will never fail you; so you can trust him to guide you in reaching your dream.

Another way God will assist you is by making wisdom available to you. The Bible tells me that 'through wisdom is a house built' (Proverbs 24:3)

God's wisdom is a mighty resource available to us when we ask. It helps us make good decisions in life. If you are struggling with how to accomplish your dream, or task, and seem to be going around and around in circles, not getting anywhere, you need God's wisdom.

Creative imaginations, innovative solutions, are gifts from God. In the creation of the universe, God used wisdom. Wisdom seeks better solutions to difficulties and better ways of doing things where others accept as unavoidable. When God's wisdom flows through you, there is no task that cannot be accomplished. Through wisdom, you can overcome anything you will face on your journey to accomplishing your dream. Wisdom will ensure your success.

However, it takes humility to ask God for wisdom. A know-it-all attitude will get you nowhere

CHAPTER THREE

COURAGE

"Be strong and courageous, because you will lead these people to inherit the land I swore to their forefathers to give them"

Joshua 1:6

"All our dreams can come true, if we have the courage to pursue them"

- Walt Disney

Like any journey, the desire to accomplish your dreams will not be an easy task. Success in any endeavor is not handed on a silver platter to you where you are; you will have to sail your boat in uncharted waters to reach your desire. Uncharted waters are unfamiliar terrains filled with uncertainties. This is where most people become afraid to step out, because uncertainties create anxiety. When you are comfortable at a level you function with ease and familiarity, reaching your dreams will be impossible. A fact that everyone knows but only few have dared is that the life they dream of is on the other side of ocean.

There is always an ocean filled with uncertainty that you must cross to get to the life you dream. We will all come to a point where we get to choose whether to just live or to thrive. In other to thrive, we will have to go beyond what we are comfortable and familiar with.

Human nature tends to lean towards the path of comfort—the path of least resistance. Even when we are faced with the choice of security or uncertainty, comfort or discomfort, ease or difficulty, our brain will almost instinctively choose ease, security and comfort.

If you truly desire to accomplish your dream, you have got to realize that you cannot do it by being comfortable and at ease; you have to stretch yourself beyond your comfort zone. That means deciding to go into unfamiliar waters. Going beyond what you are familiar with is actually where we learn and grow. No one grows from a place of comfort. The seed covered by a great mount of earth pushes against the earth during germination. The larva breaks through its cocoon to emerge a beautifully colored butterfly. Suffice to say, growth requires a little discomfort. When we're afraid of discomfort, it means we are not willing to grow and more importantly, to learn.

The question we must frequently ask ourselves is: 'does my dream challenge me?' if our dreams are not challenging, we may never go beyond our limits.

Doing something for the first time is usually very frightening: walking into school and into a classroom for the first time was frightening for most people—I was livid; riding a bike or driving a car for the first time, or even flying on an airplane for the first time are experiences we can never forget. The struggles we felt at these first time experiences were heightened by our inner voices.

These are the voices that tell us; 'don't do it, you'll get hurt'; 'you're going to ridicule yourself'; 'do you think you can achieve it?'

These voices have sabotaged many people from achieving their dreams. And if you let it, it will stop you also. Do not let that negative voice in your head rob you of the opportunity to achieve your dream.

Fear is a natural and essential part of development. It is understandable to be afraid, but it is unforgiveable to use fear as an excuse for not achieving your dream. You have got to be willing to meet life with passion and fervor, and this means taking responsibility. No excuse must be good enough to stop you!

Consider again what God told Joshua: 'be strong (confident) and of good courage, for you shall cause this people to inherit the land which I swore to their fathers to give them. Only you be strong and very courageous....'(Joshua 1:6,7)

I believe God saw through Joshua; his hesitations about his ability to succeed as Moses' replacement. Joshua, thinking about all that Moses, the great Prophet had accomplished doubted himself.

Hesitations and self-doubt are the initial obstacles we must overcome, and to do that, we require courage. It takes courage to push against the emotional turbulence of leaving our comfortable rut. What most people do not realize is that our comfort zone gets us stuck and stagnant while providing us with some false sense of safety. If your desire is to make your life count, you must be willing to take risks. Refuse to be contented with just sailing through life impervious to your true potentials.

If you want your dreams to come true, you need to take action; not someday, but right now. Unfortunately, many will not realize their dreams in life because they are too scared to try. They prefer to be spectators watching others do what they are afraid to do.

The fear of failure and the unknown is paralyzing. However, you need to face your fears if you want to achieve your dreams. You will never know what is at the end of the road until you step out and start walking.

Many years ago, I read a book—THE ALCHEMIST—by Paulo Coelho. In this book, a young shepherd boy, Santiago, undertakes a quest to traverse the world in order to find treasure and personal legend. As he draws to the end of his journey, he discovers his treasure was right where he started. He recognized his walk across the world has filled him with wisdom and a great deal of knowledge because of the people he met along the way.

Suffice to say, the young shepherd gained much experience in his quest for treasure.

What relevance is this story, you may wonder? Let me put this simply: as you journey towards your dreams, every step, every failure and every effort adds to your experience. You see, experience comes not by much idle observation or reading, but by taking simple steps into the unknown.

In order to reach your dreams, you must be willing to push beyond your personal boundaries. Everyone who have achieved their goals and reached their current level of mastery has pushed past their personal boundaries of comfort. You too must do the same if you wish to accomplish your dreams.

Stepping out of your zone of comfort is about taking risks; the larger picture here is that this journey is all about learning and growth. This is how experience is gamed. I find the story of the 'Prodigal son' very fascinating as well as educating. The story goes like this:

'Jesus went on to say, "There was once a man who had two sons. The younger one said to him, 'Father, give me my share of the property now.' So the man divided his property between his two sons. After a few days the younger son sold his part of the property and left home with the money.

He went to a country far away, where he wasted his money in reckless living. He spent everything he had. Then a severe famine spread over that country, and he was left without a thing. So he went to work for one of the citizens of that country, who sent him out to his farm to take care of the pigs.' (Luke 15:11-15, GNT)

The point I wish to draw attention to is the youngest son's resolve and courage to break from familiarity. He decided to take a risk by stepping out into the world. Although, he made bad investments owing to wrong decisions that cost him all he had, he however, gained experience that made him wiser.

The lessons he learnt by stepping out of his comfort zone, his elder brother did not have that benefit. We grow in experience only by crossing the line of certainty and familiarity. John F. Kennedy said, 'there are risks and costs to action. But they are far less than the long-range risks of comfortable inaction.'

In order to live a compelling future, you are required to take action. Taking action requires courage—the courage to take risks, whether small or big. You must take consistent action in spite of your fears and doubts. Do not be like the majority who would rather not take risks in the event that things do not turn out as they had hoped. Life is for the courageous! Only courageous people accomplish their dreams. Taking the first leap is the most crucial step in the journey to making your dream a reality.

Train yourself to ignore those negative little voices in your head as you move towards your fears. When you stop letting fear and anxiety hold you back, will you begin to make meaningful breakthroughs in life.

There will be times when you experience negative outcomes, do not let it discourage you. In fact, take every negative outcome as part of the learning process. The idea is to keep moving forward; so do not give in to your fears, and do not retreat.

You will come to realize like I have, along with everyone else who have achieved their goals, that the difference between those who fail at reaching their goals and those who succeed is courage.

The distance between where you are presently and what you desire to accomplish is courage. You have to courageously move in the direction of your dream. One thing about a dream is that it has the potential to expand a person's life. Knowing this should be enough reason to courageously pursue your dream for there is nothing as joyful as the crystallization of a dream.

CHAPTER FOUR

CONFIDENCE

"Be strong and very courageous..."
Joshua 1:7

Having faith in God is an essential part of the equation. The other part is having faith in yourself. You need both in the realization of your dream.

Success or failure is not determined by intelligence. One could have enormous intelligence and still fail. One could also have all the opportunities and resources to accomplish anything and still fail. The power to accomplish your dreams comes from taking actions based on what you believe you are capable of. This, I truly believe, is the bedrock of success in any undertaking.

A firm belief in oneself and ability are vital to success. How far you go with your dream is determined by how much you are willing to believe in yourself.

A belief in oneself is fundamental to one's capacity to achieve a dream. Norman Vincent Peale said, 'believe in yourself! Have faith in your abilities! Without a humble but reasonable confidence in your own powers, you cannot be successful or happy.'

God's presence and all the promises in scriptures would mean nothing if you lack confidence. Your success or failure in achieving your dreams comes down to this one thing—BELIEVING IN YOURSELF.

Believing in yourself increases your chances of achieving your dreams.

Think about this for a moment: if you do not believe in yourself and in your abilities to accomplish a dream, how would you expect others to believe in you?

So you see, the first investment towards actualizing a dream must come from you—you must believe in yourself.

When you move confidently in the direction of your dreams, other people will have faith in you and your ability to achieve your dream. This was what God meant when He commanded Joshua to be STRONG.

When it comes to realizing your dreams or goals, having faith in God is one essential part of the equation, the other part, is having faith in yourself. You actually need both parts to achieve a dream or whatever you sense in your spirit that God is calling you to do. A fundamental truth I want you to know is that God cannot help you beyond the level of faith you have in yourself; He cannot go beyond the limit you place on your potentials.

Believing in yourself means you are motivated to get things done. Self-confidence is vital; without it you will always be second-guessing yourself and will never achieve anything. How much do you want to achieve your dreams? Why do you want it? If you cannot honestly answer these questions with a burning desire, it means, you will not be powerfully drawn to achieve it. If you are serious about pursuing your dreams, you must go at it with conviction and certainty.

Does this mean you will not encounter tough situations or even make mistakes? You will certainly encounter difficult situations and make so many mistakes as you go about achieving your dreams. The mistakes you make along the way are just a natural part of life that you must learn to handle with the right attitude; otherwise, it may erode your confidence.

When Moses—the deliverer of Israel, was much younger, he allowed one mistake erode his confidence. Moses sensed that God was leading him to deliver Israel, but he went about it the wrong way—he killed an Egyptian. That mistake drove him into the wilderness and kept him there for 40 years doing something else. As far as his dream of leading Israel was concerned, he was through with it.

Now, at 80 years, God came to Moses in a burning bush. Guess what God told him? God did not speak to him about his mistake; there was no mention of that at all. God told him that he is sending him to Pharaoh.

However, Moses replied, 'who am I that I should go to Pharaoh?'

Moses' response showed a lack of confidence which was the result of the mistake he made earlier. His self-esteem had been eroded.

It is erroneous to think you are being humble when you think very low about yourself. The fulfillment of your assignment, the accomplishment of your goals, dreams and visions, are dependent on your self-confidence. When you lose your confidence, it becomes almost impossible to reach your dreams.

When God puts a dream in your heart it is because He believes you can achieve it. All He asks is that you believe it too. What you believe about yourself will determine whether or not you will achieve your dream. If you believe you can, then you can; but if you believe you cannot, you cannot and you will have no one to blame.

Self-doubt will prevent you from achieving your goals. If you do not believe you can, you will not. Your dreams are never possible until you begin to see them as reality. You must condition your mind to believe that your dreams are possible, that you can achieve them. Envisioning yourself achieving your dreams is a vital part of conditioning the mind.

I believe that God has given everyone the capacity to dream big, but the majority of people do not achieve their dreams because they are convinced they are incapable of achieving great things; so they settle for far less than their true potential.

Self-belief is the firm confidence that you are capable of becoming a better version of yourself. Unfortunately, this strength is lacking in the majority of people simply because whenever they attempt to accomplish something, they give up easily after encountering the first few problems. A person's self-confidence erodes with defeat.

In order to achieve your dreams, you have to intentionally work to change the fabric of your thoughts. What you habitually think determines what you will ultimately become. Your thoughts create the environment and condition that makes success or failure possible.

James Allen said, 'All that a man achieves and all that he fails to achieve is a direct result of his own thoughts.'

Once you create an environment of success by thinking success and believing in your ability to achieve a dream, success becomes an inevitable. Naturally, all the best athletes I know condition themselves mentally, emotionally and physically before every major competition. They understand that if they do not generate the right thoughts to create an enabling environment for success, they will fail. In the same way, you have to re-arrange your thoughts if you must succeed in actualizing your dream.

No man can succeed beyond the environment he creates by his thoughts. Every thought has its origin in what you believe. When you believe the wrong things it makes it difficult to succeed at anything. Those who do not believe they could ever achieve their dreams are usually correct. I may sound a bit Harsh? But that is the truth.

The Bible instructs us to renew our minds (Romans 12:2). Our thoughts and beliefs are vital to success. Renewing the mind is all about getting our beliefs right. When our beliefs are right, especially about ourselves, success is easily attainable. The journey to accomplish your dream may scar you, but you will heal—trust me. The things you will experience will definitely change you, but you should not let it erode your confidence or self-worth.

Never lose yourself when you make mistakes or even beat yourself too hard that you start wondering who you are. Every time you lose your confidence, always look to God's word and deep within yourself to recall who you are. Do not let a failure or a mistake define who you are.

This is one truth I consistently and intentionally drive into my children, especially Samantha, my second child. I let her know that she can accomplish anything in the world if she can believe enough that she can. I say this here to you; never stop trying because of a failure or a mistake. When you realize that life is a journey for which you will make some wrong turns, foolish decisions and stupid mistakes, your perspective will change.

It is always important to remember who you are. Constantly remind yourself who you are. I tell myself every day that I am the one God entrusted with a dream because He knows I can do it! Jesus said, 'if you can believe, all things are possible to him that believes' (Mark 9:23)

This is a powerful truth and I urge you to meditate on it. You can accomplish anything if you can only believe you can.

You have greater resilience than you give yourself credit. No matter what life throws at you, you can work through it. Believing in yourself is necessary if you want to succeed at your dream. If you do not have faith in yourself or your ability, just anyone who does not like you or your dream will bring you down and make you give up on your dream.

More than half the battle in anything challenging is with yourself; more than half is won if you can believe in yourself. With self-confidence, you can push through anything, and turn the tides in your favour.

Having faith in oneself is a very important quality in successful people. This quality helps one see things from a positive healthy perspective. You will see challenges as opportunities to learn, and notice more options on what you can do to move forward. Believe you can achieve your dreams and you will!

CHAPTER FIVE

DISCIPLINED-FOCUS

"Make sure you can carry out the revelation that Moses commanded you, every bit of it. Do not get off track, either to the left or right, so as to make sure you get to where you are going"

Joshua 1:7, MSG

Don't waste time on things that will not change the quality of your life.

I sat down with my kids on a weekend to watch an episode of their favorite cartoon—Princess Sofia the first. I love cartoons; I find them most educative.

Anyway, this particular episode was about Princess Sofia in Elvenmor. Sofia and Clover (the rabbit) wandered off into 'whispering woods' in search of fairies or pixies. They came across a silver tree, it was so shiny. As they went over to the tree, Clover, leaned against a hollow spot, and fell in. Sofia peeked through the hole, and saw Clover hanging onto a vine, a pit below.

Clover swings over, and as Sofia grabbed him, she slipped, and got dragged down too. As they both fell, they passed through a door, into Elvenmoor, the Elf world. An Elf named Elfonso introduced himself to them and told them where they were.

Sofia was surprised to learn that the door through which they came moves. Elfonso told them, 'the door moves several times a day. It zips down the path to other parts of Elvenmoor. But it's a long trip to the next stop, so it gives you a warning before it moves.'

What kind of warning? Sofia asked. 'It chimes a few minutes before it zips away to its next stop'. But it just got here, so we're good to go for a while', Elfonso said, Elfonso.

Back in the human world, the workers constructing the new road are planning to cut down the silver tree. If the tree is cut down, the door to Elvenmoor will be lost forever! No one will be able to get in or out!

Meanwhile, back in Elvenmoor, the door opened and another Elf named Elfred entered trying to bring Sofia news about the decision the construction workers had reached about cutting the tree. But, Elfonso interrupted him; 'can't you see we're about to go down the silver spay stream?' He led Sofia and Clover into the log. 'Don't worry, you have plenty of time for a ride', he said. No sooner had they got into the log than a sprout of water blasted the log up into the sky. They were held up there for a moment, than the sprout turned into a stream, carrying them back down. The stream curled and loop-de-loop, sending them on quite a ride.

As Elfred watched, the door started chiming, and then flew off down the road. Elfred ran over to Sofia when the stream settled.

'So, what did you want to talk to us about, Elfred? Sofia asked.

'Your royal road construction crew wants to chop down the silver tree in whispering woods, said Elfred. 'if they do, we Elves won't be able to leave Elvenmoor, and you won't be able to go home!'

I'll go back right now, and tell Dad not to cut down the tree! Sofia declared, as she got out of the log.

They ran back to where the door was, only to find it was no longer there.

'Where is the door?' Sofia asked.

'It moved', Elfred declared.

'But, I thought we had time!' Sofia stated.

'The wonders of Elvenmoor can be very distracting.' Elfred remarked. 'With all the fun to be had here, it's hard to focus on what actually matters'

Amazing story, don't you think? Well, the world around us is just like Elvenmoor; it is saturated with unlimited interruptions, with so many voices clamoring for attention.

Our world is a constant feed of information and entertainment; Newspapers, Magazines, Television, Internet. Our smartphones, the product of technological breakthrough makes it easier to connect to family and friends anywhere in the world. We get e-mails straight to our phones, and with pop up notifications from facebook, whatsapp, instagram, etc, it is so difficult to focus on what is truly important.

There are so many distractions all around, and our ability to focus and accomplish our dream suffers significantly. The ability to concentrate; the ability to focus all your attention on the task at hand is going to determine how fast you are going to achieve it, and whether or not you finish it.

I want you to understand that God designed you to be impactful, productive and fruitful, and to do that, you cannot afford to sign up for everything that knocks on your door.

In order to succeed at achieving your dream, it helps to be able to keep your attention focused on your dream, to not allow 'things' or people derail your progress. Unfortunately, most people have a hard time focusing on achieving their dreams because there are too many things distracting them along the way.

Now, think about it: how many things have distracted you in the course of reading this book?

People put off dreams or goals to a later date, or even abandon them just to attend to some other matters. The idea behind this is that they feel they have enough time.

What most people fail to understand is that Time is a finite and constantly diminishing resource. No matter how much you wished you had enough Time, it is always too short. When you grasp the brevity of Time, it will help you in managing it wisely.

Living purposefully is a decision informed by wise time management. You have got to live each day of your life with a sense of urgency knowing that your assignment and dreams must be accomplished within the span of your life here on Earth.

The Bible states; 'we must do the work of Him that sent me while it is day: for night cometh when no man can work' (John 9:4)

The 'night' speaks about a latter part in a man's life when he will have no stamina or strength to accomplish anything. This latter part of most people's lives are filled with regrets—the regrets that they did not do what they should have done when they had the time and energy.

If you truly want to live the life that counts, you will have to make the most of the opportunity you have been given TODAY. You cannot afford to spend your time drifting through life engaging in irrelevant things; time is ticking away. The stewardship of time is perhaps your greatest responsibility.

With all the distractions around us, we can easily spend valuable time, energy and resources on the things that have nothing to do with our dreams. When we are constantly distracted, we will never get things done. This is the reason God told Joshua, 'do not turn to the right or to the left'.

Our capacity for success in any field of endeavor lies not so much with our intelligence but, with our ability to focus. A constant derailing from what is important will diminish impact. It is always important to evaluate our lives at the end of each day; we must genuinely ask ourselves: 'What have I achieved today? Am I a step closer in accomplishing my dream? Did I accomplish everything I had planned on my to-do-list? Did I make the best use of my time today? Did I make progress with my dream?

Evaluations like these will help us build our priorities around our goals; it will enable us become intentional by focusing our time on what is a priority to us every day.

Most people seem to confuse being busy with being effective. One can be very busy with so many things but very ineffective. Effectiveness is measured by focusing on priority.

I find the story of Mary and her sister Martha very interesting. Jesus paid a visit to the sisters and their brother, Lazarus. As host, Martha hurried to ensure the preparations. Mary on the other hand, simply sits at the feet of Jesus to listen to words of wisdom. Martha then says to Jesus, 'Lord don't you care that my sister has left me to do the work by myself? Tell her to help me!' But, Jesus replied, 'Martha, Martha, you are worried and upset about many things, but only one thing is needed. Mary has chosen what is better, and it will not be taken away from her' (Luke 10:38-42)

A normal day for people like Martha is a series of distractions. Where you have not decided what is important to you, you will give attention to everything. The lesson of that story is about priority. You must decide what is important to you and then give it your undivided attention. You see, what you choose to focus your attention on, will determine your level of influence and impact.

There is nothing that defeats purpose like a broken focus. One quality of great achievers is the ability to focus on a goal. They focus on their goal and work towards making it a success. A focused person is like a dog with a bone; it does not drop it until it gets the marrow and every last juice.

I read a story of a Zen master and his students. One day the Zen master wanted to show his students a new technique of shooting an arrow. He told his students to cover his eyes with a cloth and then he shut his arrow. When he opened his eyes, he saw the target with no arrow in it and when he looked at his students, they looked embarrassed because their teacher had missed.

The Zen master asked them, 'what lesson do you think I intend to teach you all today?' They answered, 'we thought you would show us how to shoot at the target without looking'. The Zen master said, 'No, I taught you that if you want to be successful in life, do not forget the target. You have to keep an eye on the target'.

The ability to finish what you have started is important to your overall success. In order to achieve your goal or dream, you must perfect the ability to forget everything else but the goal. Forget all the distractions around you for a while, until you complete what you need to.

The art of focusing on our goals often requires a tunnel vision. Unfortunately, so many people are so caught up with the many things going on in their surroundings.

Rid yourself of all distractions for your success depends on it. It is not the many things you do that really matters in the end; it is the one thing you do that counts. Your ability to focus on the one thing until it is accomplished will be the distinguishing factor. I want you to understand that at any point in your life, you have to decide what is important to you. The chances for success and impact are increased significantly when you focus on one thing par time.

Impact is the result of unbroken focus.

Most people often work with the illusion that they can handle two or more tasks simultaneously. If you try doing too many things at once, you probably will not finish those tasks to a high standard. You hinder your productivity by multi-tasking.

You see, doing one thing may not make sense on the surface, but it is the ultimate path to effectiveness. If you do not focus on doing one thing at a time you are not going to achieve much.

So many things will pull you in different directions each day; but you must keep the main thing the main thing. Keep your eyes on the main thing.

Every great athlete knows the importance of keeping their eyes on the prize. From start to finish, they lay all distractions aside; they do not look back, or turn around to notice anyone on the stands. They set their minds focused on finishing and winning the race. A momentary loss of focus can cost them the race.

The British games of 1954 in Vancouver demonstrate how a split second distraction can be costly.

The race featured two runners who had both run the mile in under four minutes. Landy held the world record, and he was actually winning this race when he made one critical mistake. He looked back over his shoulder to check Bannister's position. As he looked over his shoulder on the left, Bannister surged by him on the right winning the race by 0.8 seconds.

God's instruction to Joshua was clear: 'Don't get carried away—keep looking forward' (Joshua 1: 7, GNT)

The prize is in front of you, not behind you, and certainly not beside you. So keep your gaze straight. Sometimes it is so easy to get caught up with all our achievements that it becomes a distraction. It is important to celebrate a win, but it is wrong to dwell on it. In the words of John C. Maxwell, 'don't dwell on yesterday's victory. If your focus is on what is behind you rather than what is ahead, you will crash'.

Yesterday's success can become a hindrance to Today's win when you keep focusing on it. Never plateau on your accomplishments today because there are many more dreams to actualize, and many more wins to celebrate.

Paul, the Apostle wrote, 'But one thing I do; forgetting what is behind and straining toward what is ahead, I press on toward the goal to win the prize for which God has called me heavenward in Christ Jesus' (Philippians 3:13,14)

Regardless of his past victories, Paul's focus was always on what lied ahead. The point here is not to be preoccupied with the events of the past. No one moves forward by constantly looking back.

Focus requires discipline. If you are not disciplined you cannot push against distractions. Self-discipline is the ability to do what you should be doing. It means putting off every other thing in favor of the task at hand.

When you have to work on your dream every day, trying to focus while something is notifying you of an incoming mail, tweet or messages is impossible. It takes discipline to lay aside your smart phone to avoid distractions until you have accomplished what you need to.

The objective of focus is to get more done without distractions.

CHAPTER SIX

GIVE IT YOUR ALL

"You are going to lead this people to inherit the land that I promised to give their ancestors. "GIVE IT EVERYTHING YOU HAVE, HEART AND SOUL"

[Joshua 1: 7, MSG]

"Those at the top of the mountain did not fall there"

-unknown

What do you think hurts more: the pain of hard work or the pain of regret? An overwhelming majority of people I have come across in the course of ministering are crushed by the weight of regrets. These regrets come from thinking about how things would be different today if they had only tried harder.

'if only I had paid more attention to my studies, I would have graduated with better grades' ; if only I had prepared better for that job interview, I would have had that dream job'.

Do these statements sound familiar or resonate with you? While some people regret not reaching their full potential, others regret not becoming the person they feel they could have become. If only they had all tried enough!

Unfortunately, 'if only I had tried' is the one mistake you can never go back and fix, though you can fix almost any mistake. It would have been easy to fix if only you had a 'Time-travel machine', but you and I know that this life is not science fiction movie.

In order to reach your full potential; to become the person you aspire to be, and to realize your dreams, it will require hard work. Hard work is the price we must pay to achieve our dreams.

No dream no matter how grandeur will magically manifest without hard work. Success requires hard work. If you are not willing to put in the required time, energy and work into attaining your dreams, then you will fail to get your desired outcome.

Consider the following scriptures:

"Seest thou a man diligent in his business? He shall stand before kings; he shall not stand before mean men" –Proverbs 22:29

"He becometh poor that dealeth with a slack hand; but the hands of the diligent maketh rich" –Proverbs 10:4

"The hand of the diligent shall bear rule; but the slothful shall be under tribute" –Proverbs 12:24

One quality that guarantees desired outcomes is diligence. It is the quality of the successful and prosperous. Diligence is the steady application in business.

A diligent person sees what needs to be done, and does it, and does it until he gets the desired outcome.

Success follows a process, and the accomplishment of your dream must follow the process. This process doesn't involve "a-get it now scheme", it encourages hard work though it may take a longtime.

Unfortunately, I see more and more young people in this generation who do not want to wait too long for anything-they do not want to follow the process. They want to reach their goal faster and acquire things in such a short time without willing to put in the work.

The fastest way to worthwhile success and prosperity is hard work. Mountain hikers put in the time and energy in the climb. Climbing is the process they follow to get to the top of the mountain. When they get to the top, there is a joy that overwhelms them.

The true joy of success and accomplishment come from knowing that you followed the process regardless of the obstacles you faced and how long it took.

In reality, nothing goes for nothing; you cannot accomplish something just by wishing for it or just desiring it, something is demanded and it must be given.

Life operates by giving up something to get something in return. When you think about it, all things come at a price. You can achieve anything and have anything you desire as long as you are willing to pay the price for it. It is simply how life works; it cannot be avoided. If you really want that dream in your heart to succeed, then you must be willing to pay the price required to make it a success. People who fail at reaching their dreams are unwilling to pay the price.

God's charge to Joshua was; 'you are going to lead this people to inherit the land that I promised to give their ancestors. "GIVE IT EVERYTHING YOU HAVE, HEART AND SOUL" [Joshua 1:7, MSG]

This means in other for Joshua to accomplish his task, he is going to have to put in work that is above and beyond his normal capability.

No matter what it is you want to accomplish, without giving it your ALL, You will not succeed. It is important that you give your dreams or task your ALL. You cannot expect a great result by putting in a half-hearted effort.

When you look back in retrospect and realize that you could have done more, that is an awful feeling you will have to live with and could have lived without. There is nothing more satisfying than knowing that you gave all into everything you did.

When you do more than your normal capabilities, you will increase your success and improve your result. Life rewards those who work at it. The fulfillment of your dream demands your full efforts; Make every action count.

Your dreams will remain unfulfilled and your life will not count until you are totally committed to making you dream a reality.

Giving it everything will require that you give up short-term gratification. If you are serious about accomplishing your dreams and making your life count, then you must be willing to let go of immediate gratification that might very well sabotage it.

Succeeding at attaining your dreams is dependent on your commitment to eliminating all distracting activities that could sidetrack you from your ultimate destination. If you are serious about your dreams, then you must be willing to let go of the small distracting pleasures that might well sabotage you.

This level of commitment to attaining your dream requires making personal sacrifices. Never forget that the attainment of dream or goal is not without a price. Are you willing to make the necessary sacrifices to achieve your dream?

A sign that indicate you have not made adequate sacrifices for the dream you want to achieve is the fact that you continue to sabotage your efforts on a daily basis. This might come in the form of being too busy, making excuses, indulging in procrastination, or simply being unwilling to give up certain commitments or responsibilities. You see, all these will later manifest in your life as regrets.

Anything that is worthwhile achieving in this world requires uncommon dedication and hard work. It requires considerable effort, thought and time invested in accomplishing tasks and acquiring the necessary knowledge, skills, and experience that will help you to achieve your desired dream.

You must make up your mind whether or not you are willing and able to pay the price of hard work and dedication required for the success of your dream. The decision is yours to make!

Your dreams will remain unfulfilled and your life will count very little until you begin to commit to making the necessary sacrifices of hard work and uncommon dedication.

CHAPTER SEVEN

LEVERAGE PEOPLE

"Whatever you have commanded us we will do, and wherever you send us we will go. Just as we fully obeyed Moses, so we will obey you. Only may the LORD your God be with you as he was with Moses"
(Joshua 1:16-17, NIV)

If you have seen the LORD OF THE RINGS, then you would be familiar with Frodo Baggins, the Hobbit. Frodo's mission to destroy the ring involved a treacherous journey and countless dangers. However, his task involved much more than a perilous journey to Mordor. His real challenge was to bear the ring without giving into its temptation.

Frodo could not have got through this mission without Sam. Sam gave Frodo what he needed the most to complete the quest-Hope. Without Sam, Frodo's journey would have been simply impossible. Sam was such a strong support all the way.

This brings me to an important point: success in any undertaken is not the work of one person. No one succeeds alone. So regardless of your dream, goals or project you need the help of others. To pull yourself up and forge your own path is noble but you have to realize that hardly does anyone do it alone. Ask anyone who has achieved anything worthwhile and they will tell you that somewhere along the journey they were inspired, encouraged or mentored toward their succeeding.

We are never meant to go through life alone; two, the Bible says, are better than one, because they have a good reward for their toil. For if one fall, one will lift up his fellow... (Ecclesiastes 4:9-10, ESV). We all need the community of sincere friends to spur us in reaching our dreams. Encouragement from a loving friend is vital to your success. There are times when you have to battle the feelings of insecurity, discouragement, doubt and fear, you will need someone who will come along side you speaking words of assurance; just the right words to get you back on your feet and running again.

We all need someone who will give us that extra push. If you have ever been encouraged by someone, you know how a life-giving word from a sincere friend can give you the strength to push through tough obstacles.

A genuine friend-one who sincerely loves you-will not only encourage you when you need it but, will also criticize you when that is needed. Constructive criticism from a loving friend is actually meant to straighten us up when we deviate or err just like the Bible says 'faithful are the wounds of a friend' (Proverbs 27:6)

No matter your talent or proficiency, nobody succeeds alone no more than a child can grow and learn in isolation. If you must succeed in making your dream a reality, you will need the help of other people. You have to learn how to leverage on other people's skills, experience, talent, intelligence and education.

Joshua had to enlist the support of the people. They said to him, "Whatever you have commanded us we will do, and wherever you send us we will go. Just as we fully obeyed Moses, so we will obey you. Only may the LORD your God be with you as he was with Moses" (Joshua 1:16-17, NIV)

You may have a great vision or idea, but without the support of people, you will not go far. No matter how anointed you are, or how intelligent or talented you are, you cannot succeed alone.

Jesus Christ, the son of the living God, as anointed as he was still needed people to help him with his vision. The Bible says:

"When Jesus had called the twelve together, he gave them power and authority to drive out all demons and to cure diseases, and he sent them out to preach the kingdom of God and to heal the sick" (Luke 9:1, NIV)

"After this the LORD appointed seventy-two others and sent them two by two ahead of him to every town and place where he was about to go" (Luke 10:1, NIV)

You will never go far with your dream alone. The days of the 'lone ranger' are over. No man has the monopoly of wisdom or knowledge. What this means is that you may be very good in an area, but you cannot be good in all areas. There are people who are better than you in other areas. Wisdom demands that you enlist their help to succeed.

Think about the following:

God gave Moses the vision, but he could not have succeeded without an Aaron, as well as the tribal elders of the people who helped him to mobilize the whole Israelites. And when he was going to build the tabernacle of worship, he enlisted the help of certain men who were skilled in making the furnishings for the place of worship.

Gideon was tasked with delivering Israel from the Midianites, but he couldn't have succeeded without the help of the three hundred soldiers.

When Saul was anointed the first King of Israel, there were certain men whose hearts God touched to help him.

Wherever you are presently working, your skill, intelligence, knowledge or expertise is being leveraged for the success of that organization.

I want you to understand that personal efforts are multiplied by leveraging on other people's skills, intelligence, wisdom, knowledge, talents and success.

9 798889 092582

Printed by Libri Plureos GmbH in Hamburg,
Germany